D0835387

Main-Dish
Tarts and Gratins

Little Vegetarian Feasts

Main-Dish Tarts and Gratins

Martha Rose Shulman

Author of *Little Vegetarian Feasts: Main-Dish Grains*

Illustrations by Debbie Drechsler

Bantam Books

NEW YORK TORONTO LONDON SYDNEY AUCKLAND

Little Vegetarian Feasts
Main-Dish Tarts and Gratins
A Bantam Book/June 1993

Grateful acknowledgment is made for permission to reprint the Greek Piecrust recipe, copyright © 1990 by Diane Kochilas. From the book *The Food and Wine of Greece* and reprinted with permission from St. Martin's Press, Inc., New York, N.Y.

Text and Recipes copyright © 1993 by Martha Rose Shulman
Illustrations copyright © 1993 by Debbie Drechsler
Jacket and Interior design copyright © 1993 by B. W. Honeycutt and David Albertson
Produced by The Miller Agency, Inc.
Typeset by DesignerType

Library of Congress Cataloging-in-Publication Data

Shulman, Martha Rose.
Little vegetarian feasts. Tarts and gratins/Martha Rose Shulman.

p. cm.
ISBN 0-553-08774-6
1. Pies.   2. Vegetarian cookery.   I. Title.
TX773.S435   1993

641.8′2 — dc20   92-18042
                                                        CIP

Published simultaneously in the United States and Canada

Bantam Books are published by Bantam Books, a division of Bantam Doubleday Dell Publishing Group, Inc. Its trademark, consisting of the words ''Bantam Books'' and the portrayal of a rooster, is Registered in U.S. Patent and Trademark Office and in other countries. Marca Registrada. Bantam Books, 1540 Broadway, New York, New York 10036.

Printed in THE UNITED STATES OF AMERICA
0   9   8   7   6   5   4   3   2   1

Main-Dish
Tarts and Gratins

Contents

Gratins

Introduction

Savory tarts and gratins, with their rich, familiar flavors, are an effortless way to ease into vegetarianism. The two are actually one and the same. A savory tart (or quiche) is simply a gratin baked in a crust. Gratins get their name from the French word *gratter*, to scratch or scrape. Originally gratin referred to the crusty bits that stick to the sides and bottom of a baked dish, which are so delicious to scrape away and eat. Now the word refers to a dish that forms a golden crust on the top (and often on the sides too) when baked. The crust is usually the result of a top layer of cheese (Gruyère or Parmesan) or buttered or oiled bread crumbs, or a combination of the two, browning in a hot oven. But a simple béchamel or milk-egg combination, without the addition of cheese or bread crumbs, will also brown nicely when baked long enough.

Practically anything can go into a tart or gratin. Main dish tarts usually consist of a combination of cooked vegetables, cheese, eggs, and sometimes milk; they can also be made with tofu. Traditional French quiches usually contain cream, but for low-fat richness I blend low-fat or skim milk with a couple of tablespoons of spray-dried skim milk.

You have a choice of piecrusts here. There is an almost traditional butter crust, made with half whole wheat flour. Then there are two much lower-fat olive oil crusts, one yeasted, the other not. If you don't want to bother making a crust at all, use Greek phyllo dough, which you can find in Greek markets and imported-food stores. Your crusts will be crisp and delicious and so easy to make.

Gratins can be made with raw or cooked vegetables as well as cooked pasta (macaroni and cheese is the ultimate American gratin) or grains. Lasagne is actually a gratin, as are crêpes baked in the oven with a béchamel or cheese topping. Potato gratins usually begin with uncooked potatoes, which cook in milk or stock for 1½ to 2 hours. But many of the gratins in this collection start with cooked vegetables, sometimes mixed with béchamel and sometimes not, and need only 20 to 30 minutes of cooking time. They're a great vehicle for leftovers (as are tarts), and I always find them elegant.

Let this sampling be a start. The possibilities for tarts and gratins are endless. Serve them with a big salad and a good bottle of wine and eat leftovers for lunch. Leftover tarts can also be cut into small squares or diamond shapes and served hot or cold as hors d'oeuvres.

Basic Recipes

Whole Wheat Pie Crust

Makes 1 12-to 14-inch crust

This whole wheat crust is actually half whole wheat flour and half unbleached white. It has a rich, nutty flavor and crumbly texture.

> 1 cup whole wheat pastry flour
> 1 cup unbleached white flour
> ¼ teaspoon salt
> 1 stick (8 tablespoons) cold unsalted butter, cut into small pieces
> 2 to 3 tablespoons ice-cold water as needed

1. Combine the flours and salt in a bowl or a food processor.

2. Cut in the butter using a fork, 2 knives, your hands, or the pulse action of a food processor. (To use your hands, take up bits of the mixture with both hands and rub between your thumbs and first 2 fingers. When the butter is evenly distributed through the flour and the mixture resembles oatmeal, rub the mixture briskly between your palms until it resembles coarse cornmeal.)

3. Add enough water to allow you to gather the dough together easily in a ball. Press together, without working it too much, and wrap in plastic wrap. Refrigerate for several hours or overnight. (The dough can be frozen at this point. It will keep for a month.)

4. Remove the dough from the refrigerator and let it sit for about 45 minutes before rolling it out. Place the dough on a lightly floured piece of wax paper, sprinkle a little flour over the top of the dough, and pound it a few times with a heavy rolling pin to flatten it out a bit. Now sprinkle flour over the dough and place another piece of wax paper on top. Roll out the dough until it will fit a 12- or 14-inch tart pan. Peel off the top piece of wax paper and invert the dough into the pan. Carefully pull off the bottom piece of wax paper.

5. Where the dough should ease into the edges of the pan, it is bound to break. Just press the broken edges together. Pinch a pretty lip around the top of the tart pan. The dough can be refrigerated or frozen at this point. It should be brushed with egg and prebaked for 5 minutes or so in a 350- to 375-degree oven, as directed in the recipes, before being filled and baked.

Greek Pie Crust

Makes 2 12-inch crusts

This recipe, from Diane Kochilas's *The Foods and Wines of Greece* (St. Martin's Press, 1991), is a wonderful low-fat crust made with olive oil. The dough is rolled very thin and has a crisp, bready quality.

> 2 to 2½ cups unbleached white flour or half
>   unbleached white and half whole wheat
>   or whole wheat pastry flour as needed
> 1 teaspoon salt
> 2 teaspoons baking powder
> ¾ cup water
> 3 tablespoons olive oil

1. In a bowl, mix together 2 cups of the flour, the salt, and the baking soda. Make a well in the center and add the water and olive oil. Mix together with a fork (or use an electric mixer with the paddle), until the ingredients are combined.

2. Turn the dough out onto a lightly floured surface and knead for 5 to 10 minutes, until smooth. Add remaining flour only as necessary to keep the dough from sticking.

3. Cover the dough with a slightly damp towel or wrap it in plastic wrap and refrigerate for 1 hour or up to 3 days. The dough can also be frozen for up to a month.

4. Remove the dough from the refrigerator 30 minutes

before rolling it out. Divide it into 2 equal pieces. Roll out each piece into a thin 12- to 14-inch round. Line lightly oiled tart pans with the dough and brush the surface with olive oil. Prebake for 5 minutes at 350 degrees before filling or as directed in the recipes.

PHYLLO

Phyllo dough, sometimes referred to as strudle dough, is paper-thin dough used in Greek and some Eastern European pastry. It's made in the United States by several manufacturers and is easy to find in gourmet food stores. Phyllo dough usually comes in 1-pound packages consisting of several cornstarch-dusted sheets of dough that are stacked, folded in half, and rolled up. It should be refrigerated and can be frozen. A 1-pound package of dough will give you enough sheets for two tarts.

When you use phyllo dough, keep the dough covered with a slightly damp towel as you work with individual sheets, so that it doesn't dry out and become brittle. The sheets of dough are brushed with a small amount of butter or olive oil, then layered and topped with a filling. More dough is then layered over the top. When it bakes, it becomes delicate, crisp, and delicious.

Yeasted Olive Oil Pastry

Makes 2 12-inch crusts

This is a light, crunchy pastry, very easy to work with and relatively low in fat. It rolls out very easily.

1 teaspoon active dry yeast
¼ cup lukewarm water
1 egg, at room temperature
¼ cup olive oil
1 cup whole wheat pastry flour
1 cup unbleached white flour
½ to ¾ teaspoon salt to taste

1. Dissolve the yeast in the water and let sit for 5 to 10 minutes. Beat in the egg and the olive oil. Combine the flours and salt and stir in (this can be done in an electric mixer; combine the ingredients using the paddle, then switch to the kneading hook). Work the dough only until it comes together in a coherent mass, then shape it into a ball. Place in a lightly oiled bowl, cover with plastic wrap, and let rise in a warm spot for 2 hours or a little longer. It will not rise too much, but it will expand and soften.

2. When the pastry has risen and softened, punch it down gently and divide into 2 equal pieces. Shape into balls, cover with plastic wrap, and let rest for 10 minutes. Roll out thin and line 2 lightly oiled tart pans with it. Pinch an attractive lip around the edge of the dish. Cover loosely with a dish towel and let rest for 15 minutes. Prebake for 5 minutes at 350 to 375 degrees before filling, as directed.

Béchamel

This basic white sauce is a key ingredient in many gratins. It doesn't have to be overly rich. Two tablespoons butter or oil, or a combination, will suffice for 3 cups béchamel, and low-fat or skim milk makes a perfectly creamy sauce.

> **3 cups skim milk**
> **2 tablespoons unsalted butter or olive oil or**
> **a combination**
> **2 tablespoons unbleached white flour**
> **salt and freshly ground pepper to taste**
> **pinch of freshly grated nutmeg (optional)**

1. Bring the milk to a simmer in a saucepan. Meanwhile, heat the butter and/or olive oil in a large heavy-bottomed saucepan over medium heat. When it begins to bubble, add the flour. Whisk together and cook over medium heat, stirring constantly, for a couple of minutes. Do not allow the mixture to brown.

2. Remove the pan from the heat and whisk in the milk all at once. Return the pan to the heat and bring the sauce to a simmer, stirring constantly with a whisk. When the sauce begins to thicken, reduce the heat to low and simmer the sauce, stirring often and being careful not to let it stick to the bottom of the pan and burn, for 15 to 20 minutes, until the sauce has a smooth, creamy consistency and no trace of a floury taste. Add the salt, pepper, and nutmeg, then remove from the heat.

NOTE: The béchamel can be covered and held in the refrigerator for up to a day. Place a sheet of plastic wrap over the surface of the sauce. A skin may form on the top, but this can be whisked away when you reheat the sauce.

Tarts

Greek Spinach and Leek Pie

Serves 6

This simple pie is based on the popular Greek spanakopitta. It's bursting with tasty spinach and vibrant fresh herbs.

2¼ pounds fresh spinach, stems removed and leaves well washed
1 tablespoon olive oil
3 large leeks, white part only, cleaned and thinly sliced
leaves from 1 large bunch flat-leafed parsley
2 tablespoons chopped fresh rosemary or 2 teaspoons crumbled dried
¼ cup chopped fresh dill
1½ teaspoons fresh thyme leaves or ¾ teaspoon dried
3 eggs, beaten
5 ounces feta cheese, crumbled (1 scant cup)
salt and freshly ground pepper to taste
¼ teaspoon freshly grated nutmeg
9 sheets of phyllo dough (page 16) plus olive oil to brush them
1 egg white, lightly beaten

1. Wilt the spinach over medium-high heat in a large non-aluminum frying pan in the water left on the leaves after washing. It will take about a minute for all the spinach to wilt after the water on its leaves reaches a boil. Transfer to ⟫➔

a colander and press out as much water as possible. When the spinach is cool enough to handle, wrap it in a towel and squeeze out more water. Set aside.

2. Preheat the oven to 375 degrees. Heat the olive oil in a skillet over medium heat and add the leeks. Sauté for about 10 minutes, stirring often, until softened and just beginning to brown. Remove from the heat.

3. Chop the parsley in a food processor. Add the spinach and chop fairly fine. Transfer to a bowl and stir in the remaining herbs, the leeks, eggs, feta cheese, salt, pepper, and nutmeg. Taste and adjust seasonings.

4. Brush a 12-inch tart pan with olive oil and layer in 4 sheets of phyllo dough, placing them not quite evenly on top of each other so that the edges overlap the sides of the pan all the way around. Brush each sheet with olive oil before adding the next sheet. Top with the spinach mixture. Fold the edges of the dough over the spinach mixture and brush them with olive oil. Layer 5 more sheets of dough over the top, brushing each sheet with olive oil, and crimp the edges into the sides of the pan. Brush the top with beaten egg white. Pierce the top of the pie in several places with a sharp knife. Bake for 45 to 50 minutes or until the top is golden brown. Serve hot or at room temperature.

CaBBage and ONioN TaRt with CumiN

When onions and cabbage are cooked together for any length of time, the mixture takes on a heavenly sweet flavor. Cumin seeds add an unexpected spicy touch.

> 1 olive oil piecrust of your choice (page 14 or 17)
> 1 tablespoon olive oil
> 2 medium-size onions, chopped
> 2 pounds (1 medium-size head) Savoy cabbage, shredded (about 8 cups)
> ½ cup water (or more as necessary)
> 1 cup béchamel (page 18)
> 2 eggs, beaten
> 1 teaspoon cumin seeds, crushed if desired
> salt and freshly ground pepper to taste

1. Preheat the oven to 375 degrees. Prebake the piecrust for 7 minutes.

2. Heat the oil over medium heat in a heavy-bottomed non-stick pan and add the onions. Cook, stirring often, until they soften and begin to brown around the edges, about 5 minutes. Add the cabbage and stir together for a few minutes. Add the water and cook, stirring often, for 15 minutes, until the cabbage is tender and the onions are slightly colored. If the mixture becomes dry and begins to stick to the pan, add a few tablespoons of water. Remove from the heat and transfer to a bowl.

3. Stir the béchamel, eggs, and cumin seeds into the cabbage mixture. Season with salt and pepper. Turn the mixture into the prebaked piecrust.

4. Bake for 40 minutes, until the top is slightly browned and a knife inserted in the center comes out clean. Serve hot, warm, or at room temperature.

Goat Cheese and Fresh Herb Tart

Serves 6

This marvelous combination is positively creamy, though it has no cream at all.

> 1 Greek piecrust (page 14) or 9 sheets of
>   phyllo dough plus olive oil to brush them
> 4 eggs, beaten
> ¾ cup skim milk
> 2 tablespoons nonfat dry milk
> 6 ounces fresh, not too salty goat cheese,
>   such as St. Maure
> 2 garlic cloves, minced or put through a
>   press
> 1 cup chopped fresh herbs, such as parsley,
>   basil, tarragon, chervil, dill, chives
> salt and freshly ground pepper to taste

1. Preheat the oven to 350 degrees. If you're using the Greek piecrust, roll out the crust to fit a 12-inch tart pan. Brush with a small amount of the beaten eggs and prebake for 5 minutes. If you're using phyllo dough, layer 5 sheets in the pan, brushing each sheet lightly with olive oil.

2. In a blender or food processor, blend together the skim milk and dry milk. Add the eggs, goat cheese, and garlic and blend together. The mixture should have a creamy consistency. Stir in the herbs. Add salt and pepper.

3. Turn the filling into the pastry. If you're using phyllo dough, layer the remaining sheets on top, brushing each lightly with oil. Bake for 40 minutes or until cooked through and a knife inserted in the middle comes out clean. Remove from the heat, allow to cool for about 10 minutes (or longer; this is good at room temperature as well), and serve.

Winter Squash Pie

Serves 6

I was amazed and delighted to discover this delicacy at a symposium on the foods and wines of Greece.

3 pounds pumpkin, butternut, acorn, or
   other hard winter squash, cut into halves
   or large wedges, seeds and membranes
   removed
leaves from 1 bunch flat-leaf parsley,
   chopped (optional)
2 tablespoons chopped fresh sage
2 tablespoons chopped fresh mint
¼ teaspoon freshly grated nutmeg
5 ounces feta cheese, crumbled (1 scant cup)
2 ounces Parmesan cheese, grated (½ cup)
1 tablespoon olive oil
2 large or 3 medium-size red or yellow
   onions, chopped
2 large shallots, chopped
2 large garlic cloves, minced or put through
   a press
2 eggs
salt and freshly ground pepper to taste
9 sheets of phyllo dough, plus olive oil to
   brush them
1 egg white, slightly beaten

1. Steam the squash for 15 minutes, until tender. Remove from the heat and, when cool enough to handle, cut away the skins. Place in a bowl and mash with the back of a wooden spoon or a fork. Stir in the herbs, nutmeg, and cheeses.

2. Preheat the oven to 375 degrees. Heat the olive oil in a nonstick frying pan over medium-low heat and add the onions and shallots. Sauté, stirring, until just about tender, about 5 minutes. Add the garlic and continue to sauté, stirring, for another 5 minutes or until the onions are thoroughly tender and beginning to turn golden. Remove from the heat and add to the squash. Stir in the eggs, salt, and pepper. Taste and adjust seasonings.

3. Brush a 12-inch tart pan with olive oil and layer in 4 sheets of phyllo dough, placing them not quite evenly on top of each other so that the edges overlap the sides of the pan all the way around. Brush each sheet with olive oil before adding the next sheet. Top with the squash mixture. Fold the edges of the dough over the squash mixture and brush them with olive oil. Layer 5 more sheets of dough over the top, brushing each sheet with olive oil, and crimp the edges into the sides of the pan. Brush the top with the beaten egg white. Pierce the top of the pie in several places with a sharp knife. Bake for 40 to 50 minutes, until the top is golden brown. Serve hot or at room temperature.

Leek and Potato Tart with Thyme or Cumin

Potatoes and leeks always make a good combination. Here you have a choice of thyme or cumin for the seasoning. The thyme tastes sort of Provençal, the cumin Middle Eastern.

> 1 pound (4 medium) new potatoes, diced
> 1 tablespoon unsalted butter
> 3 leeks, white part only, cleaned and thinly sliced
> ½ teaspoon dried thyme or 1 teaspoon cumin seeds, slightly crushed
> salt and freshly ground pepper to taste
> 3 eggs
> 1 piecrust of your choice (pages 12–17)
> 3 ounces Gruyère cheese, grated (¾ cup)
> 2 tablespoons freshly grated Parmesan cheese
> ⅔ cup low-fat milk
> 2 tablespoons nonfat dry milk

1. Steam the potatoes until tender, about 10 minutes, and set aside.

2. Heat the butter in a heavy-bottomed nonstick skillet, add the leeks, and saute over medium heat until they begin to soften, about 3 to 5 minutes. Add the thyme or cumin, the potatoes, and a little salt and pepper. Add a tablespoon or »→

two of water if the ingredients are sticking to the pan. Stir together over medium-low heat for 3 to 5 more minutes, until the leeks are thoroughly tender. Remove from the heat.

3. Preheat the oven to 375 degrees. Beat one of the eggs and brush the piecrust with it. Prebake the crust for 7 minutes and remove from the oven. Line the crust with the leek and potato mixture, then sprinkle with the cheeses.

4. Blend together the milk, dry milk, and remaining eggs in a blender. Add about ½ teaspoon salt and some pepper. Pour the milk mixture over the vegetables and cheese. Bake for 30 minutes or until the top is just beginning to brown and a knife inserted in the middle comes out fairly clean. Remove from the heat and serve immediately or cool and serve at room temperature.

Garlicky Tomato Tart

Serves 6

This tart always reminds me of summer in Provence, where lots of garlic and tomatoes go into every meal. If you have no great summer tomatoes, use canned ones and omit the sliced tomatoes. The tart is best if it sits for about 15 to 20 minutes before being served.

> 1 piecrust of your choice (pages 12–17)
> 4 eggs, at room temperature, beaten
> 1 tablespoon olive oil

3 to 4 large garlic cloves, minced or put
   through a press
1 pound (4 medium-size) ripe tomatoes,
   peeled, seeded, and chopped
1 tablespoon tomato paste
salt to taste
1 teaspoon fresh thyme leaves or ¼ to ½
   teaspoon dried, to taste
1 tablespoon chopped fresh basil
freshly ground pepper to taste
⅔ cup low-fat or skim milk
¼ pound Gruyère cheese, grated (1 cup)
1 ounce Parmesan cheese, grated (¼ cup)
2 large tomatoes, sliced crosswise about ¼
   inch thick

1. Preheat the oven to 350 degrees. Brush the bottom of the crust with some of the beaten egg, and prebake the crust for 5 minutes.

2. Heat the olive oil in a heavy-bottomed saucepan or non-stick skillet over low heat. Add the garlic and cook, stirring, for 30 seconds to a minute, until fragrant and beginning to color. Add the chopped tomatoes, tomato paste, and salt and cook over medium-low heat, stirring, until you have a fairly thick paste, about 20 minutes. Stir in the thyme, basil, and pepper and adjust seasonings. Remove from the heat.

3. Beat together the milk and remaining eggs. Stir in the tomato mixture and cheeses.

4. Line the bottom of the partially prebaked crust with the sliced tomatoes. Pour in the tomato mixture. Bake for 45 minutes or until a knife inserted in the middle comes out clean. Let sit for 15 to 20 minutes before serving.

Ratatouille Tart

Serves 6

Ratatouille, the fragrant Provençal vegetable stew, makes a wonderful filling for a tart. Make it a day ahead of time for best results. If there are no good ripe tomatoes, canned tomatoes are fine.

> 1 large eggplant (about 1 pound), cut in
>   half lengthwise
> 2 tablespoons olive oil
> 2 medium-size onions, sliced
> 4 large garlic cloves, minced or put
>   through a press
> 1 red bell pepper, sliced
> 1 green bell pepper, sliced
> 1 pound (4 medium-size) ripe tomatoes,
>   peeled, seeded, and cut into wedges
> salt and freshly ground pepper to taste
> 1 bay leaf
> 1 teaspoon dried oregano
> 3 tablespoons chopped fresh basil or 1 to 2
>   teaspoons dried
> 1 pound (3 small or 2 medium-size)
>   zucchini, sliced about ¼ inch thick
> 2 ounces Gruyère cheese, grated (½ cup)
> 1 ounce Parmesan cheese, grated (¼ cup)
> 1 piecrust of your choice (pages 12–17)
> 3 eggs, beaten

1. Preheat the oven to 450 degrees. Score the cut side of the eggplant and place it cut side down on a lightly oiled baking sheet. Bake for 20 minutes or until shriveled. Remove from the heat, allow to cool, and dice.

34

2. Heat 1 tablespoon of the olive oil in a large heavy-bottomed casserole over medium-low heat and add the onions and half the garlic. Sauté, stirring, until the onion is tender, about 5 minutes. Add the remaining oil and the peppers and eggplant. Continue to cook, stirring, over medium-low heat for about 10 minutes, until the peppers and eggplant are beginning to cook through. Add the tomatoes, remaining garlic, salt, pepper, bay leaf, and dried herbs. Continue to cook over low heat, stirring the vegetables from time to time, until they have released quite a bit of liquid.

3. Raise the heat to high, give the vegetables a stir so that they don't stick to the bottom of the pan, and bring to a boil. Reduce the heat, cover partially, and simmer for 45 minutes, stirring occasionally. Add the zucchini and more salt and pepper if desired, and cook for another 15 to 20 minutes. Stir in the fresh basil if you're using it and adjust the seasonings.

4. Place a colander over a bowl and place the ratatouille in the colander. Drain for 15 minutes. Transfer the liquid in the bowl to a saucepan and reduce over high heat to ½ cup. Stir the liquid back into the ratatouille. Add the cheeses.

5. Preheat the oven to 350 degrees. Brush the piecrust with a bit of the beaten eggs and prebake for 5 minutes. Stir the remaining beaten eggs into the ratatouille and turn the mixture into the piecrust. Bake for 40 to 45 minutes, until firm. Serve hot, room temperature, or cold.

MushRoom Quiche

Serves 6

This savory "quiche" doesn't have an egg in it. When you blend tofu and bake it, it takes on a marvelous creamy consistency. This tart is good hot or cold.

> 1 piecrust of your choice (pages 12–17)
> 1 tablespoon olive or canola oil
> 1 small onion, chopped
> 3 garlic cloves, minced or put through
>   a press
> ¾ pound mushrooms, cleaned and sliced
> 2 tablespoons dry white wine
> ½ teaspoon dried thyme
> salt and freshly ground pepper to taste
> 1¼ pounds firm or soft tofu
> ½ cup plain low-fat yogurt
> 1 tablespoon unbleached white flour
> 2 tablespoons tamari or Kikkoman soy sauce
> ½ teaspoon yeast extract, such as Marmite
>   or Vegex*
> 1 tablespoon tahini
> 1 teaspoon freshly grated ginger (optional)
> 1 tablespoon fresh lemon juice (optional)
> pinch of cayenne pepper
> pinch of freshly grated nutmeg

1. Preheat the oven to 350 degrees. Brush the piecrust with a little olive oil and prebake for 5 minutes.

2. Heat the oil in a large heavy-bottomed skillet over medium-low heat and add the onion and a third of the garlic. Sauté, stirring, until the onion begins to soften.

3. Add the mushrooms and remaining garlic and cook over medium heat, stirring often, for 5 to 10 minutes, until the mushrooms are soft and have begun to release liquid. Add the wine, thyme, salt, and pepper, stir together until the wine evaporates, and remove from the heat.

4. Blend together the remaining ingredients until completely smooth in a food processor or blender. Stir in the onion and mushroom mixture and turn into the partially prebaked pie crust. Smooth the top with a spatula.

5. Bake for 40 minutes, until the top is browned and the tofu mixture is set. Remove from the oven and let cool for 10 minutes before serving.

*Yeast extract is a thick, viscous spread with a salty, savory flavor. The British produce a version called "Marmite," which is available in imported-food stores. "Vegex" is an American product sold in health food stores.

Zucchini and Red Pepper Tart

As beautiful to look at as it is to eat, this pale green and yellow tart, with splashes of red, is always a hit. It's good hot or cold. If you have one, use the French fry blade on your food processor to cut the zucchini.

> **1 piecrust of your choice (pages 12–17)**
> **3 eggs, beaten**
> **1 tablespoon olive oil**
> **2 large (about 1 pound) red bell peppers, diced**
> **2 garlic cloves, minced or put through a press**
> **1½ pounds (3 medium-size to large) zucchini, cut into julienne or French-fry-size sticks (about 5 cups julienne)**
> **salt to taste**
> **1 teaspoon fresh thyme leaves or ½ teaspoon dried**
> **freshly ground pepper to taste**
> **2 ounces Gruyère cheese, grated (½ cup)**
> **1 ounce Parmesan cheese, grated (¼ cup)**
> **½ cup skim milk**

1. Preheat the oven to 350 degrees. Brush the pie crust with a bit of the beaten egg and prebake for 5 minutes.

2. Heat the olive oil in a large heavy-bottomed skillet over medium-low heat and add the red pepper and half of the garlic. Sauté for a few minutes, stirring, until the peppers begin to soften. Add the zucchini, remaining garlic, and salt. Sauté, stirring over medium-low heat, for 5 to 10 minutes, until the zucchini is crisp-tender. Stir in the thyme and pepper and remove from the heat. If the ingredients begin to stick to the pan, add a few tablespoons of water.

3. Toss together the zucchini mixture and the cheeses in a bowl. Beat the remaining eggs and milk together, toss with the zucchini mixture, and adjust the seasonings. Transfer to the prebaked pie crust.

4. Bake for 35 to 45 minutes, until just beginning to brown on the top and a knife inserted in the center comes out clean. Serve hot or at room temperature.

GRATINS

GRiLLed EggPLaNt GRatiN

Serves 4

This is a heavenly, pungent gratin with a smoky flavor.

> 2 pounds (2 to 3 large) eggplant
> 2 to 3 large garlic cloves, minced or put through a press
> ½ cup plain low-fat yogurt
> salt and freshly ground pepper to taste
> 1 to 2 tablespoons fresh lemon juice (optional)
> 3 tablespoons chopped parsley
> 3 tablespoons fine dry bread crumbs
> 3 tablespoons freshly grated Parmesan cheese
> 2 tablespoons olive oil

1. Grill the eggplants, turning often, under a broiler, on a ridged top-of-the-stove grill, or on the barbecue until soft and uniformly charred. Remove from the heat, place in a bowl, cover tightly, and allow to cool.

2. Peel the eggplant and discard the liquid that has accumulated in the bowl. Mash in a food processor fitted with the steel blade, in a mortar and pestle, or with a fork, and ⟫⟶

stir in the garlic, yogurt, salt, pepper, and lemon juice if you're using it.

3. Preheat the oven to 400 degrees. Oil a 2-quart gratin dish and spread the eggplant puree in the dish. Mix together the parsley, bread crumbs, and Parmesan and sprinkle the mixture over the eggplant. Drizzle on the olive oil and bake for 30 to 40 minutes, until the top is browned. Serve hot.

Jerusalem Artichoke Gratin

Serves 4

Jerusalem artichokes really do have a flavor reminiscent of artichoke hearts. Their texture, however, is much softer. The peas are necessary here for color, and they add sweetness to this marvelous, fragrant dish. The ground-nut topping makes a rich addition to the dish, but you have a choice; plain bread crumbs are good, too.

> **2 pounds Jerusalem artichokes**
> **juice of ½ lemon**
> **1½ cups shelled fresh peas, steamed for 5**
> **to 10 minutes until tender, or thawed**
> **frozen peas**
> **salt and freshly ground pepper to taste**

2½ tablespoons olive oil
½ pound not-too-salty fresh goat cheese
⅓ cup low-fat milk or plain yogurt, or a
   combination
2 garlic cloves, minced or put through
   a press
1 teaspoon fresh thyme leaves or ½
   teaspoon dried
6 tablespoons fine dry bread crumbs or 2
   tablespoons ground hazelnuts or almonds
   mixed with ¼ cup bread crumbs

1. Preheat the oven to 450 degrees. Oil a 1½-quart gratin dish. Peel the Jerusalem artichokes, cut them into ½-inch-thick pieces, and place in a bowl of water acidulated with the lemon juice to prevent discoloration.

2. Drain the artichokes and toss with the peas, salt, pepper, and 1½ teaspoons of the olive oil in the prepared dish.

3. In a food processor fitted with the steel blade or in a bowl using a wooden spoon, blend together the goat cheese and the milk and/or yogurt until smooth. Add the garlic and thyme and lots of pepper. Spread this mixture over the Jerusalem artichokes and peas. Sprinkle on the bread crumbs or crumb-and-nut mixture. Drizzle on the remaining olive oil.

4. Bake for 15 minutes, until the bread crumbs are browned and the dish is sizzling. Serve hot.

Baked Orecchiette with Broccoli and Tomato Sauce

This gratin is an updated version of macaroni and cheese. If you can't find orecchiette—literally "little ears"—use elbow macaroni or penne.

2½ tablespoons olive oil
3 garlic cloves, minced or put through
  a press
2½ pounds (about 10 medium-size)
  tomatoes, peeled, seeded, and chopped
pinch of sugar
salt to taste
2 tablespoons chopped fresh basil or ½
  teaspoon dried thyme or oregano
freshly ground pepper to taste
½ pound orecchiette noodles
1 bunch (about 1½ pounds) broccoli, broken
  into small florets
3 ounces Parmesan cheese, grated (heaped
  ¾ cup)
2 tablespoons fine, dry whole wheat
  bread crumbs

1. Heat 1 tablespoon of the oil in a large heavy-bottomed skillet or saucepan over medium-low heat. Add a third of the garlic and cook until it begins to color, about 30 seconds. Add the tomatoes, remaining garlic, sugar, and salt. Bring to a simmer and cook, stirring often, for 15 minutes. Add the herbs, more salt if desired, and the pepper. Cook for a few minutes longer and remove from the heat.

2. Preheat the oven to 400 degrees. Oil or butter a 3-quart gratin dish.

3. Bring a large pot of water to a boil. Add a teaspoon or more of salt and the orecchiette. Boil for 8 minutes and add the broccoli. Cook until the pasta is cooked through but still firm to the bite, another 4 to 5 minutes. Drain and toss with the tomato sauce and ½ cup of the cheese; transfer to the gratin dish. Mix together the remaining cheese and bread crumbs and sprinkle it over the pasta mixture. Drizzle on the remaining oil.

4. Bake for 20 to 30 minutes, until the top begins to brown and the gratin is bubbling. Serve hot.

Savory Baked Noodles

Tofu can be blended into a creamy, nutty sauce that goes beautifully here with whole wheat or buckwheat noodles. When it bakes, it firms up like a custard.

> 1 pound firm or soft tofu
> 1 tablespoon dark miso paste
> 1 tablespoon tamari or Kikkoman soy sauce
> ½ cup plain low-fat yogurt
> ¼ cup water
> 2 tablespoons tahini
> 2 tablespoons dry sherry
> pinch of freshly grated nutmeg
> pinch of cayenne pepper (optional)
> 2 ounces Parmesan cheese, grated (½ cup; optional)
> 1 teaspoon salt
> 10 ounces whole wheat or buckwheat noodles

1. Preheat the oven to 350 degrees. Oil a 2- or 3-quart gratin dish. Begin heating a large pot of water.

2. When the water reaches a rolling boil, add the salt and noodles. Cook al dente and drain.

3. Meanwhile, blend together the tofu, miso paste, soy sauce, yogurt, water, tahini, sherry, nutmeg, and cayenne, if you're using it, until completely smooth in a food processor or blender. Taste and adjust seasonings. Stir in the Parmesan cheese.

4. Toss the noodles with the tofu mixture and turn into the gratin dish. Bake for 45 minutes, until the top is beginning to brown. Remove from the oven, let stand 5 to 10 minutes, and serve hot.

Potato Gratin with Sage

Serves 6 to 8

In the Auvergne region of France, potato gratins are made with stock instead of milk (they add crème fraîche, too). It makes for a savory dish, especially with the addition of sage. Fresh sage is much better than dried here. You can peel the potatoes or not, according to your taste.

2 large garlic cloves, cut in half lengthwise
1 teaspoon unsalted butter or olive oil
3 to 3½ pounds small russet or new
  potatoes, scrubbed and sliced about
  ¼ inch thick
2 tablespoons slivered fresh sage leaves or
  2 teaspoons dried
salt (about ¾ teaspoon) and freshly ground
  pepper to taste
¼ pound Gruyère cheese, grated (1 cup)
2 eggs, beaten
4½ cups vegetable or chicken stock

1. Preheat the oven to 400 degrees. Rub the inside of a large (about 14 by 9 by 2 inches) oval gratin dish all over

with the cut garlic and brush with the butter or olive oil. Rub again with the garlic, slice the garlic thinly, and toss with the sliced potatoes and sage. Add salt and lots of pepper. Place half the mixture in an even layer in the gratin dish. Sprinkle on half the cheese and repeat the layers. Beat together the eggs and stock and pour the mixture over the potatoes; it should nearly cover them.

2. Place the gratin in the middle of the oven and bake for 1½ to 2 hours, until the top is brown and crusty. During the first hour, every 20 minutes or so, remove the casserole from the oven and break up the top layer of potatoes that is getting dry and crusty, give the potatoes a stir, and return to the oven. Serve hot.

Endive Gratin with Walnuts

Serves 4

I put everything I love in an endive salad into this fragrant, nutty combination.

> 8 large (1½ to 2 pounds) Belgian endives
> ½ cup water
> salt and freshly ground pepper to taste
> 2 ounces Gruyère cheese, grated (½ cup)
> ¼ cup broken walnut pieces (about 10 walnuts)
> 2 tablespoons chopped fresh parsley
> 2 tablespoons walnut oil

1. Preheat the oven to 400 degrees. Oil a 1½- or 2-quart gratin dish.

2. Cut the bottoms off the endives and cut them in half lengthwise. Remove the bitter inner cores. Cut crosswise into 1-inch slices. Place in a pot with the water and bring the water to a boil. Add salt, reduce the heat, cover, and simmer for 10 minutes. Drain and toss with pepper and more salt if desired. Place in the prepared gratin dish.

3. Combine the cheese, walnuts, and parsley and sprinkle over the endives. Drizzle on the oil. Bake for 20 minutes, until the top is browned and the gratin bubbling. Serve hot.

Provençal Summer Gratin

Make sure you have sweet ripe tomatoes for this beautiful, garlicky gratin.

> 4 large (about 2 pounds) red bell peppers
> 6 large (about 2 pounds) ripe tomatoes,
>   peeled and cut in half crosswise
> ¼ teaspoon sugar
> salt and freshly ground pepper to taste
> 4 large garlic cloves, minced
> 2 ounces Gruyère or Parmesan cheese,
>   grated (½ cup)
> ½ cup chopped parsley
> ¼ cup bread crumbs (fresh or dry, whole
>   wheat or white)
> 2 tablespoons olive oil

1. Roast the peppers over a gas flame or under a broiler, turning until they are all uniformly charred. Seal in a plastic bag or wrap in a clean kitchen towel and allow to cool. Remove the charred flesh when cool enough to handle, rinse, and pat dry. Cut in half lengthwise, and remove the seeds and membranes. Cut each half lengthwise into 2 pieces and set aside.

2. Preheat the oven to 325 degrees. Oil a gratin dish large enough to accommodate all the tomato halves. Line with the roasted peppers.

3. Gently squeeze out the seeds from the tomato halves. Place, cut side up, on top of the peppers in the gratin dish. Sprinkle with sugar, salt, and pepper. Mix together the garlic, grated cheese, parsley, and bread crumbs; sprinkle the mixture over the tomatoes. Drizzle on the oil.

4. Bake for 45 minutes, until the topping is brown and crisp. Serve hot, with rice or pasta.

Zucchini and Garlic Gratin

For some reason this pale green garlicky gratin tastes much richer than it actually is. Serve it sizzling and hot.

> 3 pounds (6 medium-size) zucchini, grated
> salt to taste
> 2 tablespoons olive oil
> 6 large garlic cloves, minced or put through
>   a press
> 3 tablespoons chopped parsley
> 1 teaspoon fresh thyme leaves or ½
>   teaspoon dried
> freshly ground pepper to taste
> 2 ounces Gruyère cheese, grated (½ cup)
> 2 eggs, beaten
> 2 tablespoons fine bread crumbs (fresh or
>   dry, white or whole wheat)

1. Sprinkle the zucchini liberally with salt and place in a colander for 15 minutes. Squeeze out the moisture, rinse thoroughly, and squeeze dry.

2. Preheat the oven to 425 degrees. Oil a 1½- or 2-quart gratin dish.

3. Heat 1 tablespoon of the olive oil in a heavy-bottomed nonstick skillet over medium heat and add half the garlic. When it begins to color (after about 30 seconds), add the zucchini and remaining garlic. Cook, stirring often, over medium-low heat for 5 to 8 minutes, until the zucchini has softened and is fragrant but still bright green.

4. Add 2 tablespoons of the parsley, the thyme, salt, and pepper. Stir together and remove from the heat. Transfer to a bowl and stir in half the Gruyère and the beaten eggs. Adjust the seasonings.

5. Turn the zucchini mixture into the prepared gratin dish. Toss the remaining parsley and Gruyère with the bread crumbs. Sprinkle over the top of the zucchini. Drizzle on the remaining tablespoon of olive oil.

6. Bake for 20 minutes, until the top is browned and crusty. Serve hot.

FRaGRaNt
TuRNiP GRatiN

This dish looks a bit like a potato gratin. The garlic and thyme infuse the milk and turnips to produce an irresistibly aromatic gratin.

> 2 large garlic cloves
> 1 teaspoon unsalted butter or olive oil
> 3 tablespoons fresh or dry, fine or coarse whole wheat bread crumbs
> salt to taste
> 3 pounds medium-size turnips, peeled, cut in half lengthwise, and sliced crosswise about ¼-inch thick
> 1 teaspoon fresh thyme leaves or ½ teaspoon dried
> freshly ground pepper to taste
> 2 eggs, beaten
> 3½ to 4 cups low-fat milk (enough to cover the turnips)
> 2 ounces Gruyère cheese, grated (½ cup)

1. Preheat the oven to 425 degrees. Rub the inside of a 3-quart gratin dish with a cut clove of garlic and brush with the butter or oil. Add 1 tablespoon of the bread crumbs and tilt the dish around until the edges and bottom are lightly coated.

2. Bring a large pot of water to a boil. Add 1 teaspoon salt and the turnips, bring back to a rolling boil, and drain.

3. Thinly slice the remaining garlic clove. Toss the blanched turnips with the garlic, thyme, salt, pepper, eggs, and milk in a bowl. Turn into the prepared gratin dish and bake for 30 minutes.

4. Mix together the cheese and remaining bread crumbs and sprinkle over the top of the bubbling gratin. Return to the oven and bake for another 15 to 20 minutes, until the top is crusty and brown. Serve hot.

NOTE: This gratin will be slightly watery when you remove it from the oven, but the water will be reabsorbed after it stops bubbling.

Spinach and Rice Gratin

This Provençal dish is best eaten at room temperature or cold. It's a great quick lunch and makes wonderful picnic fare, washed down with some chilled Bandol rosé wine.

- 2 pounds fresh spinach, stems removed and leaves well washed, or 2 10-ounce boxes frozen spinach, thawed
- 3 tablespoons olive oil
- 1 medium-size onion, chopped
- 2 garlic cloves, minced or put through a press
- 1½ cups cooked rice (½ cup uncooked)
- 2 ounces Gruyère cheese, grated (½ cup)
- 2 tablespoons freshly grated Parmesan cheese
- ½ cup chopped parsley
- 1 teaspoon fresh thyme leaves or ½ teaspoon dried
- 3 eggs, beaten
- salt and freshly ground pepper to taste
- 2 heaped tablespoons fine dry bread crumbs (whole wheat or white)

1. Heat a large nonstick frying pan over medium-high heat and add the spinach. Cook, stirring, until it wilts in the water left on its leaves. It will take about a minute for all the spinach to wilt after the water on its leaves reaches a boil.

Transfer to a colander and press out as much water as possible. When the spinach is cool enough to handle, wrap it in a towel and squeeze out more water. Chop fine. If you're using defrosted frozen spinach, squeeze out the water.

2. Preheat the oven to 375 degrees. Brush a 2-quart gratin dish with olive oil.

3. Heat 1 tablespoon of the olive oil in a heavy-bottomed nonstick skillet over medium heat. Add the onion and sauté, stirring, until tender and just beginning to brown, about 5 minutes. Add the garlic and spinach. Stir together for about 30 seconds, then transfer to a large bowl. Stir in the rice, cheeses, parsley, thyme, and beaten eggs. Add the salt and pepper. Turn the mixture into the prepared gratin dish and smooth the top with the back of a spoon. Sprinkle on the bread crumbs and drizzle on the remaining oil.

4. Bake for 30 minutes or until the gratin is set and the top golden brown. Remove from the heat and allow to cool. Cover and refrigerate. Cut into squares and serve.

Potato and Roquefort Gratin

Here's another rich, comforting potato gratin, this one from the southwestern part of France, Roquefort country.

> 2 large garlic cloves, cut in half lengthwise
> 1 teaspoon unsalted butter or olive oil
> 3 to 3½ pounds small russet or new
>   potatoes, scrubbed and sliced about
>   ¼-inch thick
> salt and freshly ground pepper to taste
> pinch of freshly grated nutmeg
> 4½ cups skim milk
> 2 eggs, beaten
> ½ pound Roquefort cheese, crumbled
>   (about 1 cup)

1. Preheat the oven to 400 degrees. Rub the inside of a large (about 14 by 9 by 2 inches) oval gratin dish all over with the cut garlic and brush with the butter or olive oil. Rub again with the garlic, slice the garlic thinly and toss it with the sliced potatoes along with salt, lots of pepper, and the grated nutmeg.

2. Beat together the milk and eggs and stir in the Roquefort. Toss with the potatoes and turn into the gratin dish.

3. Place in the middle of the oven and bake for 1½ to 2 hours, until the top is golden and crusty. During the first hour, every 20 minutes or so, remove the casserole from the oven and break up the top layer of potatoes that is getting dry and crusty, give the potatoes a stir, and return to the oven. Serve hot.

Pumpkin Gratin

Any hard winter squash, such as butternut or acorn, will work for this sweet fall/winter gratin. The béchamel takes on the most beautiful pale orange color when you mix it with the squash.

> 3 pounds pumpkin
> 2 tablespoons chopped fresh sage or 1½ teaspoons dried
> salt and freshly ground pepper to taste
> 1 recipe béchamel (page 18)
> ¼ to ½ teaspoon freshly grated nutmeg to taste
> 2 ounces Gruyère cheese, grated (½ cup)
> 2 tablespoons fresh or dry, coarse or fine, whole wheat bread crumbs
> 2 teaspoons olive oil

1. Peel and halve the pumpkin and remove the seeds and membranes. Cut the squash into ¼-inch-thick slices. Steam the squash for 10 minutes, until tender. Remove from the heat and transfer to a bowl. Toss gently with the sage, salt, and pepper.

2. Season the béchamel with salt, pepper, and nutmeg. Remove from the heat and stir in the cheese.

3. Preheat the oven to 375 degrees. Butter a 2-quart gratin dish.

4. Pour the béchamel into the bowl with the pumpkin and gently toss the mixture together. Turn it into the buttered gratin dish. Sprinkle the bread crumbs over the top and drizzle on the olive oil.

5. Bake for 40 minutes or until the top is beginning to brown and the mixture is bubbling. Remove from the heat and serve hot.

METRIC CONVERSION CHART

CONVERSIONS OF OUNCES TO GRAMS

Ounces (oz)	Grams (g)
1 oz	30 g*
2 oz	60 g
3 oz	85 g
4 oz	115 g
5 oz	140 g
6 oz	180 g
7 oz	200 g
8 oz	225 g
9 oz	250 g
10 oz	285 g
11 oz	300 g
12 oz	340 g
13 oz	370 g
14 oz	400 g
15 oz	425 g
16 oz	450 g
20 oz	570 g
24 oz	680 g
28 oz	790 g
32 oz	900 g

*Approximate. To convert ounces to grams, multiply number of ounces by 28.35.

CONVERSIONS OF POUNDS TO GRAMS AND KILOGRAMS

Pounds (lb)	Grams (g); kilograms (kg)
1 lb	450 g*
1¼ lb	565 g
1½ lb	675 g
1¾ lb	800 g
2 lb	900 g
2½ lb	1,125 g; 1¼ kg
3 lb	1,350 g
3½ lb	1,500 g; 1½ kg
4 lb	1,800 g
4½ lb	2 kg
5 lb	2¼ kg
5½ lb	2½ kg
6 lb	2¾ kg
6½ lb	3 kg
7 lb	3¼ kg
7½ lb	3½ kg
8 lb	3¾ kg
9 lb	4 kg
10 lb	4½ kg

*Approximate. To convert pounds into kilograms, multiply number of pounds by 453.6.

CONVERSIONS OF FAHRENHEIT TO CELSIUS

Fahrenheit	Celsius
170°F	77°C*
180°F	82°C
190°F	88°C
200°F	95°C
225°F	110°C
250°F	120°C
300°F	150°C
325°F	165°C
350°F	180°C
375°F	190°C
400°F	205°C
425°F	220°C
450°F	230°C
475°F	245°C
500°F	260°C
525°F	275°C
550°F	290°C

*Approximate. To convert Fahrenheit to Celsius, subtract 32, multiply by 5, then divide by 9.

CONVERSIONS OF QUARTS TO LITERS

Quarts (qt)	Liters (L)
1 qt	1 L*
1½ qt	1½ L
2 qt	2 L
2½ qt	2½ L
3 qt	2¾ L
4 qt	3¾ L
5 qt	4¾ L
6 qt	5½ L
7 qt	6½ L
8 qt	7½ L
9 qt	8½ L
10 qt	9½ L

*Approximate. To convert quarts to liters, multiply number of quarts by 0.95.